Christmas Cookies & Crafts

A Collection of Recipes, Stories & Craft Ideas

Written by
RosaLinda Buchner Graziano
Illustrated by
Patricia Rosencrantz
Recipes supplied by
Maura Cooper, Chef

Brownlow

ISBN: 1-57051-385-6

Illustrations by Patricia Rosencrantz
Recipes by Maura Cooper
Stories, craft projects and decorating tips
by RosaLinda Buchner Graziano
Design by Koechel Peterson & Associates

Printed in U.S.A.

Table of Contents

1-2-3 Magic Dough Ornaments

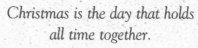

1 cup corn starch
2 cups baking soda
1 1/4 cups water

Combine 3 ingredients in medium saucepan;
bring to full boil, stirring constantly.
(Like magic, dough will form!) Cool on plate
in refrigerator for 15 minutes. Knead dough; roll
1/4" thick. Cut with cookie cutters. Use drinking
straw to make hole at top of ornament. Set aside
to dry for 2-4 days. When thoroughly dry, color
with craft paint. Decorate as desired.
String with ribbon to hang.

*Christmas is the day that holds
all time together.*

ALEXANDER SMITH

Baker's Salt Dough Ornaments

1 cup salt
2 cups all purpose flour
3/4 cup water (more/less)

Preheat oven to 300 degrees. Mix ingredients; knead 10 minutes, or until elastic. May require extra flour for kneading. Roll 3/8" to 1/2" thick for stronger cutouts; cut with cookie cutters. Can also be shaped freehand. (Don't forget to make hole at top with a straw.) Can be decorated before baking* or painted after. Bake on flour-dusted cookie trays at 300 degrees for 3 hours, or until hard. Spray with shellac. Thread ribbon through hole and hang.

*Cinnamon red-hot decorations will
melt and are not recommended
in this recipe.

Quick Icing

3/4 cup powdered sugar
1 teaspoon food coloring
3 teaspoons water

Mix in measuring cup until smooth.
Add more food coloring and less water for
darker color. Lemon juice, orange juice,
or various extracts may be
substituted for water.

Decorating Cookie Cutter Tree Ornaments

Decorating your cookie ornaments can be as simple as sprinkles and jimmies or as elaborate as glitter and lace. The following samples will help start your creative juices flowing, but don't stop there. Let your imagination go free! Improvise! Get wild! Go crazy! And have some holiday fun!

The finest Christmas gift is not the one that costs the most money, but the one that carries the most love.

HENRY VANDYKE

Heart Frame

(For use with a 4" or 5" heart-shape cookie cutter.)

Cut out large heart shape from prepared dough.
Use a smaller 2" or 3" heart-shape cookie cutter to
cut out center of large heart. With straw, poke holes
for hanging at top and bottom of large heart, and
top only of small heart. Use a toothpick to etch the
current year or child's age on front of small heart.
Decorate, paint as desired. Shellac both
pieces. When dry, glue child's photo
on back of large heart,
with picture showing through
opening. Attach small ribbon
bow just under hole in small
heart. Tie satin ribbon through
holes in bottom of large heart and
top of small heart (so small heart
dangles freely). Loop another strand of
satin ribbon through hole at top of large
heart, and hang.

Christmas Tree Ornament:

Select a dough ornament recipe. Before baking/setting, gently press cinnamon red-hots into the dough "branches" and a candy star on treetop. When cooled/set, use a small paintbrush to apply Quick Icing with green food coloring to paint the tree. Apply sprinkles while still wet, or allow to dry and zig-zag a line of glue and glitter for garland. Finish as called for in recipe.

Variation:

Glue tiny strands of red velvet, knotted in center, on branches to look like bows. Glue one larger bow at treetop. Tie a three-inch strip of red velvet through hole, and hang.

The Red Wagon

So reminiscent of Christmases past, the McKringle family tradition was an old-fashioned gift from the heart: delicious homemade cookies, delivered fresh and oven warm to the neighbors on Christmas Eve day. Their foil-wrapped, ribbon-tied gifts were stacked securely in Nicky's little red wagon while he and his seven-year-old twin sister, Noelle, pulled it through the neighborhood.

We had moved in one week earlier, when on the afternoon of December 24 three years ago, the doorbell chimed to announce our first visitor. You can imagine my delight upon finding the twins, bundled in red and green like wrapped presents, standing at the door singing "We Wish You a Merry Christmas" as they handed me one of their pretty packages.

No one knows exactly how the McKringles' cookies stayed so warm while in that little red wagon, but I like to think they were kept warm by the true spirit of friendship and brotherly love.

Cookies on a Stick

What a delicious way to spend the day!
Both Mom and kids will enjoy getting
creative with this fun and easy-to-do Christmas
craft. Whether you use a favorite sugar cookie recipe
(edible) or a dough ornament recipe (non-edible),
this project is sure to bring smiles and smiles
of merriment and cheer.

• SCRUMPTIOUS AND FUN :
Before baking your half-inch thick
cutter-cut cookie dough, gently press
lollipop sticks into the smaller shapes,
or popsicle sticks into the larger shapes.
Decorate with sprinkles, jimmies, or
sugar before baking; or dip in melted
chocolate when cooled and place on
wax paper in refrigerator.
Serve with a smile.

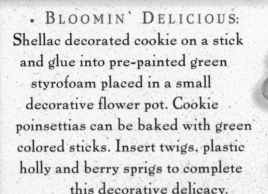

• BLOOMIN' DELICIOUS:
Shellac decorated cookie on a stick
and glue into pre-painted green
styrofoam placed in a small
decorative flower pot. Cookie
poinsettias can be baked with green
colored sticks. Insert twigs, plastic
holly and berry sprigs to complete
this decorative delicacy.

*TIP: Potted Cookies on a Stick make
wonderful get-well, cheer-up,
and hospital gifts, too!*

*"Busy Hands" Hint: Make a rainy day indoors
seem brighter by baking Smiley Faces on a stick. No
round-shaped cookie cutter? Improvise by using the
rim of an ordinary drinking glass!*

Fun 'n Kooky Cookie Jewelry

Kids not only love the excitement of Christmas, they love being part of the festivities, and making their own gifts is a great way for them to join in the fun. Cookie jewelry can be given to Grandma, Teacher, and kids alike. Don't forget to make an extra one for the class grab bag!

• Cookie Necklace: Use any prepared and decorated cut cookie, looping a strand of red, green, or white yarn through hole at top. (Gold or silver stretch string works well, too.) Add fabric swatches, like a scarf for a snowman ornament or a heart-shaped cutout from a patchwork design material, and glue onto a teddy bear ornament.

Glue lace or netting onto an angel ornament; add white pearl drops from small tube of cake decorating icing or gold glitter to her halo to make her look more "heavenly."

• Cookie Pins: Hot glue plastic pin to backside of prepared dough ornament. Wreath dough ornaments make perfect pins. Decorate with candies (for ornament balls) before baking/setting or dot with colored cake icings from cake decorating tubes after set. Paint wreath (not decorations) green with Quick Icing. Sequins or glitter make this piece of jewelry shine!

Christmas is not a date. It is a state of mind.

MARY ELLEN CHASE

The Angel Harp

Being recently married, we didn't have much money to spare for our first Christmas. So I baked several batches of dough ornaments to give as gifts and to decorate the almost four-foot tall evergreen I had purchased at the corner lot. Trying to fill in the sparseness, I carefully adorned the branches with dangling strands of tinsel and home-strung popcorn garland, knowing the treetop ornament I had fallen in love with and could not afford would have to wait until next year.

But on Christmas morning—bejeweled with red sequins and three feathery angels—the golden angel harp I had longed for lit up our tree from its lofty perch, and my heart lit up with a warm and special love for my kind and generous husband.

Many a Christmas has come and gone since then, but like our wedding rings, the angel harp remains as a solid symbol and heartfelt reminder of our young and everlasting love.

Cookie Cutter Garland

Here is a fun decoration that's a great snowy day pastime for kids! Outline a gingerbread man cookie cutter on a piece of cardboard; use scissors to cut around outline. Place cardboard cutout on brown, red, and green construction paper, and cut out 12 pieces each, totaling 36 gingerbread men. Decorate the cutouts with crayons, magic markers, and glitter. Lay the cutouts face up in any color sequence. Glue hand of one cutout onto hand of the next, to form a "hand-in-hand" chain of gingerbread men to hang on walls or pin to the draperies in your child's bedroom.

A real kid-pleaser, for sure!

Variation:

Cut 1" x 6" strips of red and green construction paper. Glue ends of one strip together to make a circle/ring. Add 6 more rings of alternating colors (7 rings total) to form a chain. Make 4 chains. Staple one chain before, after and between sets of 6 gingerbread men, for the sequence: *7 rings, 6 gingerbread men, 7 rings, 6 gingerbread men, 7 rings, 6 gingerbread men, 7 rings.* Add more or less, as desired.

He who has not Christmas in his heart
will never find it under a tree.

ROY SMITH

Cookies and Greenery

Homemade decorative touches throughout the house warm the holiday season with old-fashioned tradition. Make your own Cookie Wreath with styrofoam and plastic greenery, or add your special cookie touches to a store-bought countertop tree. Be inventive, have fun, and create a tradition this Christmas!

• COOKIE WREATH:

Hot glue smaller-size decorated cut cookies to real or artificial wreath. Add fake holly berries at random. Lace with raffia, and hang in your kitchen for a "homey" Christmas look.

Variation: In lieu of cookies, secure Christmas cookie cutter shapes to wreath, using twist ties.

• COOKIE TREE:

Any kind of small tree will do! Decorating this
tree is a real treat for the kids, especially when
you designate it to be "Their Very Own Special
Little Christmas Tree." Let the kids make and
decorate all the edible cookies, and be sure
to have plenty of spares on hand for
replacements...because eating them
is half the fun!

*TIP: Don't forget to make holes with a straw for
hanging the cookies with string.*

*"Busy Hands" Hint:
Have kids string popcorn for
tree garland as an added
kid-made decoration.*

Christmas Puppy Love

Ever since my boys were old enough to talk, they had begged for a puppy. Simple games of Frisbee or "catch" usually turned into "go fetch" as they playfully wrestled on the front lawn and giggled over which one would pretend to be the family pet. But this Christmas morning all that would change.

After we had finished opening our gifts I happened to "discover" beneath the tree, one last present with a tag that simply read "Handle with Love and Care." When the boys knelt down to open the sturdy, ribbon-tied box, the lid fell to the side; and up popped the cutest little tan-and-white fur ball of a puppy you ever did see!

As a reminder of this very special moment, the kids named him Codak, with a "C" for "Christmas." But I need only look at my boys' smiling faces to know just how special a Christmas moment can be.

Cookie Cutter Bean-y Babes

THE CRAZE CONTINUES...HOMEMADE STYLE!

Fold in half a sturdy piece of cloth material. Use your child's favorite (and largest) cookie cutter shape as a pattern to trace onto the backside of cloth. Pin both sides together along edge of shape; and cut both pieces, leaving them joined at the fold. Front of material will face each other on inside. Be sure to cut enough extra for a half-inch to one-inch inside seam. Sew together using a tight stitch; leave a two-inch opening. Turn material right-side out and fill interior with any kind of kitchen dry beans. Slip-stitch the hole closed. Trim with buttons, lace, ribbons, or simple satin stitching to create a truly lovable, huggable toy!

TIP: Cookie cutter shapes can be used for quilting pieces (baby blanket) and appliques (kid's jeans, pockets). Add a splash of scented oil, or fill with scented beads, and they make fragrant sachets for closets and drawers, too!

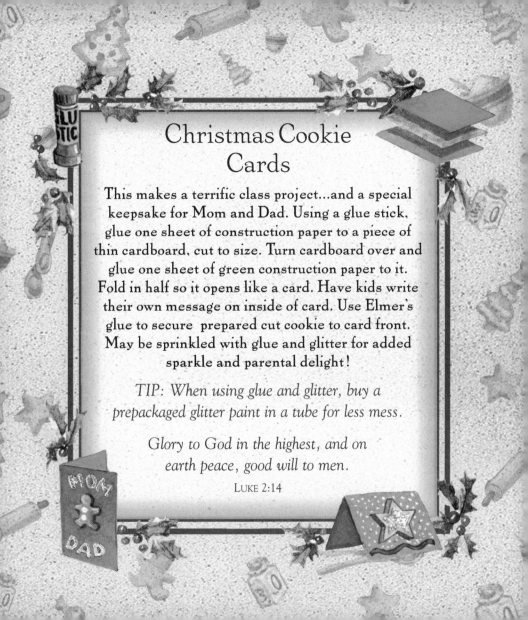

Christmas Cookie Cards

This makes a terrific class project...and a special keepsake for Mom and Dad. Using a glue stick, glue one sheet of construction paper to a piece of thin cardboard, cut to size. Turn cardboard over and glue one sheet of green construction paper to it. Fold in half so it opens like a card. Have kids write their own message on inside of card. Use Elmer's glue to secure prepared cut cookie to card front. May be sprinkled with glue and glitter for added sparkle and parental delight!

TIP: When using glue and glitter, buy a prepackaged glitter paint in a tube for less mess.

Glory to God in the highest, and on earth peace, good will to men.

LUKE 2:14

Ultimate Sugar Cookies

1/4 cup sugar, 1 cup all-vegetable shortening
2 large eggs, 1/4 cup light corn syrup
1 Tablespoon vanilla
3 cups all purpose flour, plus 4 Tablespoons divided
3/4 teaspoon baking powder
1/2 teaspoon baking soda
1/2 teaspoon salt

1. Preheat oven to 375 degrees.

2. Combine sugar and shortening in a large bowl. Beat at medium speed with an electric mixer until they are well blended.

3. Add eggs, corn syrup and vanilla. Beat together till well blended and fluffy.

4. Combine 3 cups flour, baking powder, baking soda and salt in a separate bowl.

5. Gradually add the dry mixture to the creamed one with the beaters at low speed. Mix until well blended.

6. Divide the dough into 4 equal parts.

Hint: If the dough is too soft or sticky to roll out, wrap each quarter of the dough with plastic wrap and refrigerate at least 1 hour.

7. Spread 1 Tablespoon of flour on a large sheet of waxed paper.

8. Place 1/4 of the dough on the floured waxed paper. Slightly flatten the dough with the palm of your hand.

9. Turn the dough over on the floured waxed paper and cover it with another sheet of waxed paper, then roll it out—between the two sheets of waxed paper—to 1/4 inch thickness.

10. Flour the cookie cutters to be used and cut out the dough into the desired shapes.

11. Transfer the cookies to an ungreased baking sheet with a large pancake turner, placing them 2 inches apart.

12. Sprinkle the cookies with granulated sugar or colored sugar crystals, or leave them plain to frost or decorate when cooled.

13. Bake one baking sheet at a time at 375 degrees for 5 to 9 minutes depending on the size of your cookie sheets. Smaller, thinner cookies will take closer to 5 minutes; larger cookies closer to 9 minutes. DO NOT OVERBAKE!

14. Cool 2 minutes on the baking sheets, meanwhile placing sheets of foil on the countertop. Put the cookies on the foil to cool completely.

Makes about 3-4 dozen cookies.

Hint: You can use granulated sugar, colored sugar crystals, frosting, decors, candies, chips, nuts, raisins, coconut or decorating gels—your choice of decorations.

Ginger Cookies

1 1/4 cups all-purpose flour, 2 teaspoons ground ginger
1/4 cup firmly packed dark brown sugar
1/4 cup molasses, 3 1/2 Tablespoons margarine, melted
egg white of 1 large egg, lightly beaten

1. Sift together the flour and ginger into a bowl then stir in the sugar.

2. In a separate bowl combine molasses, melted margarine
   and egg white. Stir until well blended.

3. Add the wet ingredients to the dry ingredients and combine thoroughly.

4. Cover the bowl with plastic wrap and place in the freezer for
   30 minutes or until firm.

5. Shape the dough into balls, each around 1 inch in diameter, using
   small cookie cutters to make pleasing shapes.

6. Preheat the oven to 350 degrees and lightly spray a cookie sheet with
   cooking oil spray.

7. Place the cookies on the prepared cookie sheet 1 inch apart and bake
   for 12 minutes.

8. Immediately remove the cookies from the baking sheet and place
   them on a wire rack to cool completely before decorating.

Makes 18-20 cookies.

HAVING A CHRISTMAS DINNER PARTY?

Personalize cookie cut gingerbread
man dough ornaments to use as individual
place markers. Let your guests
know this is a gift for them to
take home.

FILL A LARGE BASKET with cookie
cutters, pine cones, and
antique or ball ornaments.
Ribbon tie six cinnamon
sticks together in a pack. Attach
to basket handle and add a sprig
of greenery.

Our Family Tree

As I gaze upon my Christmas tree adorned in twinkling white lights and red velvet bows, I realize what decorates my tree are not the delicate ornaments that hang from each limb, but rather the memories each ornament brings of past Christmases shared with family and friends.

The bow-topped, mirrored gift box ornaments Mom and Dad gave to me when I was nine still reflect their parental devotion. The sets of beaded sequin ornaments I made when my girls were born still bring smiles, shiny and bright. Their school-made star ornaments still glisten with glitter. And the spun crystal ornaments collected through the years still sparkle with the spirit of friendship in which they were given.

So, as I gaze upon my Christmas tree in all its shimmering glory, I realize it is truly a Family Tree...evergreen with love.

Crisp Little Lemon Cookies

1 package pudding-in-the-mix lemon cake mix
1 cup crisp rice cereal
1/2 cup (1 stick) margarine or unsalted butter, melted
1 large egg, slightly beaten

1. Preheat oven to 350 degrees.

2. In a large bowl combine all ingredients and mix well.

3. Shape the dough into balls, 1 inch diameter each.

4. Press firmly on the dough balls to flatten them, using small cookie cutters to make pleasing shapes.

5. Place them 2 inches apart on ungreased baking sheets.

6. Bake 9-12 minutes or until light golden brown around the edges.

7. Cool 1 minute on the baking sheets before removing to wire racks to cool completely.

8. When they're thoroughly cooled, decorate as you wish.

Makes 3-4 dozen cookies.

Brown Sugar Icebox Cookies

1 cup all-purpose flour, 1/4 teaspoon baking soda
1/8 teaspoon salt, 4 Tablespoons margarine, softened
2/3 cup tightly packed, dark brown sugar
1 teaspoon vanilla, 1 large egg white

1. Combine flour, baking soda and salt in a bowl and set it aside.

2. Beat margarine at medium speed of a mixer until light and fluffy.
   Gradually add the sugar, beating at medium speed until well blended.

3. Add in the vanilla and egg white and beat till thoroughly combined.
   Add in the flour mixture and stir until well blended.

4. Turn the dough out onto waxed paper and shape it into a 6 inch long log.
   Wrap the log in waxed paper and freeze for 3 hours or until it's very firm.

5. Preheat oven to 350 degrees and coat the cookie sheet with cooking oil spray.

6. Cut the log into 1/4 inch thick slices, using small cookie cutters to make
   pleasing shapes, and place the cookies 1 inch apart on the prepared
   cookie sheet. Bake for 8-10 minutes.

7. Immediately remove the cookies and place on a wire rack to cool
   completely before decorating.

Makes 2 dozen cookies.

Chocolate Icing
for Decorating

6 ounces semisweet chocolate morsels
4 Tablespoons unsalted butter
1/2 cup heavy cream
1/4 teaspoon salt
2 cups superfine sugar
2 teaspoons vanilla

1. Combine all ingredients except vanilla in a large, microwaveable bowl and heat on high for 1 minute.

2. Stir the contents of the bowl, then heat on high for 1 minute.

3. Remove the bowl from the microwave oven and stir again to make sure everything is thoroughly mixed together.

4. Add in the vanilla.

Makes about 3 cups

*It is Christmas in the heart that puts
Christmas in the air.*

Vanilla Cream Frosting

3 Tablespoons butter at room temperature
1 teaspoon vanilla
1/4 teaspoon salt
3 cups confectioner's sugar
5 Tablespoons hot cream (but not boiling)

1. In a large bowl, blend together the butter, vanilla and salt.

2. Stir in 1/2 cup confectioner's sugar and mix well.

3. Add in hot cream and remaining confectioner's sugar alternately in small amounts, beating well after each addition.

OPTIONAL:
Start with 2 drops of vegetable food coloring,
such as red or green. Be sure to mix VERY thoroughly!
Add more, drop by drop, as desired.

*Hint: If the icing seems too soft, add more sugar
and stir to combine till stiff.*

A Kid's Christmas

When my brother Bobby and I were young, part of our Christmastime excitement was knowing we would spend a few fun-filled, jolly holidays with Grandma and Grandpa Ross.

One whole day, from early morning to early evening, would be set aside for baking cookies with Grandma in her big country kitchen. We'd sing Christmas songs as we worked our dough, and giggled each time we chased Grandpa from sneaking hot cookies when the oven bell signaled another baked batch.

At night as the yule logs crackled beneath the mantle-hung knitted stockings, Grandma would prepare hot tea and a bedtime snack of our homemade cookies, while Bobby and I nestled into Grandpa's lap as he sat in his favorite "thinking chair" and lovingly read aloud to us the story of the first Christmas from his treasured Bible.

Growing more precious with every passing year, those Christmastime memories will always hold a special place in my heart...just like Grandma and Grandpa Ross.

Attach decorative ribbon and a couple of jingle bells

to your holiday cookie cutters and hang them as ornaments on your Christmas tree, or add a bit of potpourri to a piece of netting tied in the center of the cutters and hang them in your windows.

Start a tradition! Begin a "Christmas Keepsake Journal"

and have each family member, visitor, friend, and guest write in it. Hot glue your favorite finished dough ornament to the cover for decoration. Fun to look back on as years go by!

Christmas began in the heart of God.
It is complete only when it reaches
the heart of man.

Tea Party Cookies

3/4 cup unsalted butter, 2 cups tightly packed, dark brown sugar
3 large eggs, lightly beaten, 1/2 teaspoon salt
1 teaspoon vanilla, 1 teaspoon baking soda
1 Tablespoon hot water, around 3 cups of all-purpose flour

1. Cream together the butter and sugar, then add the beaten eggs, salt and vanilla and combine thoroughly.

2. Stir the baking soda into the hot water and let it cool slightly. Add it to the creamed mixture.

3. Add 2 cups of flour to the mixture and stir until it comes together. The dough should be quite stiff; add more flour till you get it that way.

4. Lightly flour the palm of your hand and flatten the dough into a disk. Wrap the dough in plastic wrap and refrigerate it for 1-2 hours.

5. Roll out the dough to 1/8 inch thickness and cut into desired shapes with cookie cutters.

6. Preheat oven to 400 degrees and lightly spray cookie sheets with cooking oil spray. Put the cookies on the prepared cookie sheets. Bake until lightly browned, 5-8 minutes.

7. Let the cookies cool on the cookie sheets for 2 minutes before transferring them to a wire rack to cool completely, then decorate with colored sugar crystals, chips, decorating gels or icing as you wish.

Makes around 5 dozen small cookies.

Chocolate Butter Cookies

1 cup (2 sticks) unsalted butter, room temperature, 2/3 cup superfine sugar
10 ounces semisweet chocolate, grated, 1 teaspoon vanilla
1/4 teaspoon salt, 2 cups all-purpose flour

1. Cream together the butter, superfine sugar, grated chocolate, vanilla, and salt with an electric mixer until completely combined but not fluffy. Do not overmix!

2. Stir in the flour one cup at a time using a wooden spoon or a rubber spatula. Mix just until the flour is incorporated.

3. Form the dough into a log and cover it completely with plastic wrap. Refrigerate at least 2 hours or overnight.

4. Preheat the oven to 350 degrees. Line 2 baking sheets with parchment or waxed paper.

5. Remove the dough from the refrigerator and let it soften slightly before rolling it out. Divide the dough into quarters. On a well-floured work surface, roll out 1 quarter of the dough at a time to 1/4 inch thickness. Run a long metal spatula under the dough to loosen it from the surface.

6. Cut out shapes with cookie cutters as close together as you can get them. Transfer the cut dough to the prepared baking sheets with the spatula, leaving 1 inch between the cookies. Repeat with the remaining dough. Gather up all the scraps and roll them out to make more cookies.

7. Bake 15-20 minutes until the edges are lightly browned. Remove from the oven and cool on the baking sheets for 10 minutes before transferring to wire racks to cool completely before decorating. Store in an airtight container.

Makes about 2 dozen cookies.

MAKE YOUR OWN CHRISTMAS GIFT WRAP!
Using small cookie cutters, trace and cut out
shapes on sponges. Dip sponge designs into
acrylic paint and stamp onto white
shelving paper.

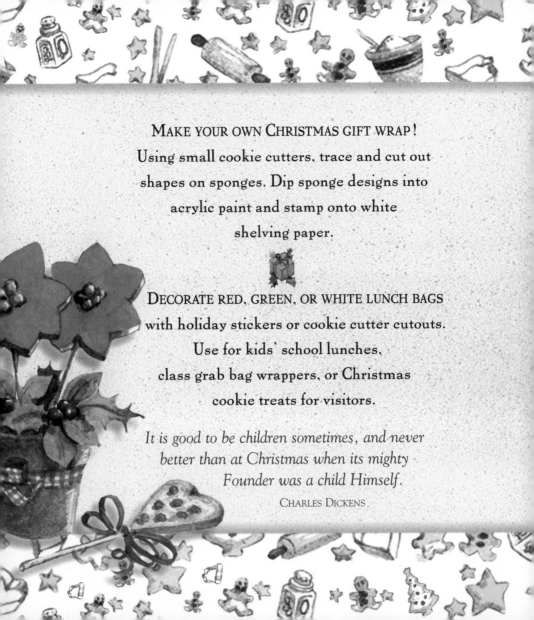

DECORATE RED, GREEN, OR WHITE LUNCH BAGS
with holiday stickers or cookie cutter cutouts.
Use for kids' school lunches,
class grab bag wrappers, or Christmas
cookie treats for visitors.

*It is good to be children sometimes, and never
better than at Christmas when its mighty
Founder was a child Himself.*
CHARLES DICKENS

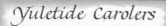
Yuletide Carolers

With just the right chill in the air and a light snowfall under way, it was a perfect night for Christmas caroling. Friends and neighbors mingled as we sang our way through the streets to my house for our annual Yuletide Carolers' Gathering of merriment and good cheer.

We toasted marshmallows in the fireplace, warmed our hands on mugs of hot cocoa, and treated our taste buds to a variety of home-baked goodies. When the piano accompanied the sweet voice of young Jenny Dodd singing "The Drummer Boy," a reverent hush fell over the crowd. Following her lead, we all joined in once again when she began to sing "Silent Night."

As my husband and I stood in the doorway, waving to the last of the carolers, we noticed the snow had stopped falling and the sky was gleaming with stars. But in the eastern sky, warming the night with its heavenly glow, one beautiful star burned silent and bright...sending a shining message of Peace, Love, and Joy.

Silent Night, Holy Night

O Little Town of Bethlehem

Hark, the Herald Angels Sing

Joy to the World

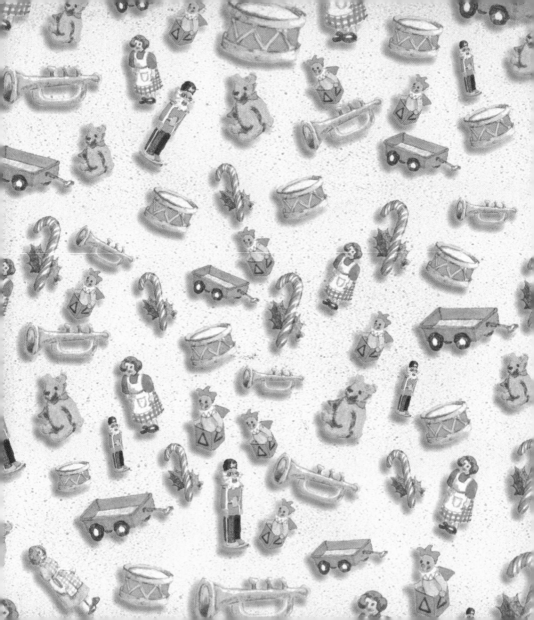